BUTTERFLIES

The chalk cliffs of the Purbeck Coast support a diverse range of flora, fauna and insect life. Here, many of the more unusual species of butterflies can be found.

LULWORTH SKIPPER ▷

A West Country speciality is the Lulworth skipper. Occurring in high density between Burton Bradstock and Studland, this insect is not to be found anywhere else in Britain.

◁ COMMON BLUE

The common blue is sadly no longer as abundant as its name suggests, but still occurs in good numbers in coastal locations around the South West.

COUNTY ORGANISATIONS CONCERNED WITH WILDLIFE CONSERVATION IN THE SOUTH WEST

CORNWALL TRUST FOR NATURE CONSERVATION,
5 ACRES,
ALLET,
TRURO,
TR4 9DJ.
Tel: 0872 73939

DEVON WILDLIFE TRUST,
188 SIDWELL STREET,
EXETER,
EX4 6RD.
Tel: 0392 79244.

SOMERSET TRUST FOR NATURE CONSERVATION,
FYNE COURT,
BROOMFIELD,
BRIDGWATER,
TA5 2EQ.
Tel: 0823 451587.

DORSET TRUST FOR NATURE CONSERVATION,
39 CHRISTCHURCH ROAD,
BOURNEMOUTH,
BH1 3NS.
Tel: 0202 554241.

WILDLIFE TRUST FOR BRISTOL, BATH & AVON,
THE WILDLIFE CENTRE,
32 JACOB'S WELLS ROAD,
BRISTOL,
BS8 1DR.
Tel: 0272 268018.

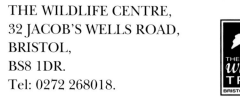

WILTSHIRE WILDLIFE TRUST,
19 HIGH STREET,
DEVISES,
SN1D 1AT.
Tel: 0380 725670.

HAMPSHIRE WILDLIFE TRUST,
8 ROMSEY ROAD,
EASTLEIGH,
SO50 9AL.
Tel: 0703 613636.

GLOUCESTERSHIRE WILDLIFE TRUST,
DULVERTON BUILDING,
ROBINSWOOD HILL COUNTRY PARK,
RESERVOIR ROAD,
GLOUCESTER,
GL4 9SX.
Tel: 0452 383333.

INDEX OF PHOTOGRAPHS

WILDLIFE IN THE WEST COUNTRY

Photographs by Colin Varndell

WILDLIFE IN THE WEST COUNTRY

Photographs copyright Colin Varndell 1994
Text copyright Colin Varndell and Nigel Clarke

First published by Nigel J. Clarke Publications in 1994

Nigel J. Clarke Publications
Unit 2, Russell House,
Lym Close, Lyme Regis,
Dorset, DT7 3DE
TEL: 01297 442513
FAX: 01297 442513

Colour transparencies covering all aspects of natural history are
available for reproduction from:
Colin Varndell,
The Happy Return,
Whitecross,
Netherbury, Bridport,
Dorset, DT6 5NH.
TEL: 01308 488341

ISBN 0–907683–4–4

Design by Nigel J. Clarke Publications.
Typesetting by DP Photosetting, Aylesbury, Bucks
Additional typesetting and design by Sue Clarke.
Additional technical advice Jim Hall.
Origination, printing and binding in Singapore,
under the supervision of MRM Graphics Ltd, Winslow, Bucks

COVER PICTURE: Barn owl in flight

CONTENTS

FOREWORD

The purpose of this book is to share some of the wonders of wildlife to be found in the West Country with its readers, and hopefully to encourage more people to take an active role in the preservation of nature by joining one of the local county trusts for nature conservation.

These bodies take on the responsibility for maintaining natural habitats for the benefit of wildlife as well as for our own enjoyment. Increased membership would mean a greater financial viability and in turn will result in a more secure future for our wildlife.

I have always enjoyed a close association with the natural world, and long before I considered photographing nature, I spent my time sitting quietly in wild places watching birds and animals going about their daily business.

This passion for wildlife, culminated in the purchase of a camera in 1976 in the hope of sharing some of my experiences with others. To begin with, my idea of wildlife photography was to wander around the woods and hedgerows, taking pictures of birds and animals as they presented themselves. This concept could not have been further from the truth, and I soon learned that successful nature photographs are the result of careful reconnaissance, meticulous planning and above all – endless patience!

Wildlife photography is fraught with setbacks and disappointments, and while the pictures in this book represent some of my more successful moments, they are only the tip of the iceberg. For every successful project, there are countless failures and fruitless long sessions spent in cramped, often cold and wet conditions. Patience and time are two essential resources which are frequently drained beyond their limits.

Over the years, many individuals have assisted me in my quest for wildlife photos. They are too numerous to mention here, but I hope that this collection of pictures will go some way towards expressing my gratitude for their help.

Working as a wildlife photographer and raising a young family do not blend together smoothly. I am extremely fortunate in that my family have always shown total support in my endeavours. My wife has been a constant source of encouragement to me, and together with my children, has made great sacrifices in order for me to obtain these photographs.

To Susy, Holly and Emily, thank you for your patience, understanding and untiring support. This book is dedicated to you.

COLIN VARNDELL.

Agricultural land forms the main habitat in the South West Region, typically consisting of open field systems divided by hedgerows and interspersed with copses, river valleys and villages.

Time has healed the wounds of man's deprivation of the wild woodland which once covered the area, giving the impression that farmland is the natural order of things.

For much of our native wildlife, open field systems are little more than hostile desert, but some birds, animals and insects have adapted well to make their livings in this man-made habitat.

BURCOMBE VALLEY ▷

◁ RABBIT

Rabbits are vegetarian and, much to the annoyance of farmers and growers, feed on the fresh shoots of grass and crops. They often make their underground burrows in open fields, which can create a hazard to both farm machinery and cattle. Despite their abundance, it is seldom possible to approach rabbits in the wild to photograph them. Even when the photographer is concealed within a hide, rabbits will still identify human scent and remain underground. This photograph was taken from an elevated hide which kept traces of my scent well above the 'nose line' of the rabbit.

BARN OWL ▷

T he eerie spectre of a barn owl gliding silently over watermeadows at twilight was once a common sight in the West Country. With a call resembling a strangled scream, this bird is steeped in superstition. Sadly the barn owl has declined to a point where it now inhabits only a few scattered locations in the region.

This photograph was taken at a baiting site on the Somerset Levels. A beam of infra red light played on to a photo-electric cell was set up across the owl's flight path. As the owl passed through the light, the photo cell emitted an electronic pulse which activated the camera shutter and fired four flashguns.

◁ BUZZARD

T he common buzzard is the most abundant diurnal bird of prey to be seen in the South West of England. Soaring on the air currents with its huge, broad wings, the buzzard is a hawk with a high profile, often acting as an ambassador for nature by attracting human attention, and even kindling an interest in birds and wildlife.

The buzzard is not an easy bird to photograph as it is wary of humans, especially those who carry cameras! This shot was taken from a hide at a baiting site where the bird was offered carrion regularly for four years before obtaining the photograph.

LITTLE OWL ▷

E ven though the little owl is often accused of just about every crime in the gamekeeper's calendar, it is not a serious predator of gamebird chicks or even of birdlife generally. The bird in fact does much good by feeding on many pests of agriculture like the cockchafer, as the picture shows.

This photograph was taken by setting up a light beam shutter triggering system at a little owl nest.

◁ MAGPIE

I n the natural world, relationships between predator and prey are important, and whilst predation must not be allowed to outpace the prey population, it must assist in keeping numbers in check to ensure there is enough food to go round. Small birds have many predators, including the magpie which will take eggs and nestlings of smaller species. Despite an apparent increase in the magpie population in recent years, there is little scientific evidence in support of the theory that magpie activity is reducing the numbers of their prey species.

WOODPIGEONS ▷

The sound of woodpigeons 'cooing' in copses and hedgerows on warm summer evenings carries far on humid air. The woodpigeon has benefited greatly from the changes which agriculture has made to the landscape, as it prefers open country where it will feed on seeds and foliage.

Indeed, this bird's liking for foliage has made it the number one bird pest for farmers and growers, as it is able to inflict heavy damage to crops by defoliating young plants.

◁ COLLARED DOVE

Unlike the nervous woodpigeon, the collared dove is an approachable species, especially when it is near to its favourite food – grain! I stalked this bird in a farmyard in winter. It was coming down for corn which had been thrown to the chickens. It was one of those days when strong sunlight was frequently interrupted by cloud. As I moved stealthily towards the bird I noticed the head and shoulders were in full sun, but the back and tail were in shade. It was therefore necessary to wait patiently for the sun to go in, so an even light may fall upon the dove.

CHAFFINCH ▷

T he chaffinch is regarded by many ornithologists as possibly the commonest breeding bird in the British Isles, although it probably shares this position with the blackbird. The chaffinch is extremely abundant in Wessex, and in winter, large flocks of chaffinches will visit artificial food supplies like garden bird tables. This male was attracted within camera range by regularly putting out mixed wild bird seed near a hide at the edge of a field.

◁ GOLDFINCH

T he goldfinch is not a keen bird tabler, but takes the seed of a variety of field-edge weeds like groundsel, burdock, dandelion and teasel. To take this photograph, I first cut some dead teasel plants from a hedgerow and stood them near my hide.

FARMLAND

CORN BUNTING ▷

O n occasions, a car can prove to be a useful hide. I had noticed this corn bunting singing on fenceposts at the side of a farm track near Langton Herring. When I drove past the bird, it remained on the post, totally ignoring my car. With my telephoto lens on my lap, I quietly freewheeled towards the bird and photographed it from the car window.

◁ REDWING

A rriving in the South West in the late autumn, often in huge numbers, the redwing shows a particular liking for holly berries. Being the smallest member of the thrush family found in the region, they may suffer during hard weather as the larger thrushes drive the redwing away from food. This photograph was taken from a hide which I had erected near a berry-laden holly tree in late November.

FOX CUB RUNNING ▷

Due to the fox's acute senses, it is necessary to devote an enormous amount of time to increase the opportunities of obtaining photographs. The adult shown here was attracted to bait in winter. The main picture of the cub running was the result of exposing many hundreds of frames before I got this one shot.

◁ FOX

Most countryfolk seem to fall into one or other of two distinct categories in their attitudes towards the fox. We either love the animal and want to protect it, or we hate the fox and wish to destroy it. Whichever side of the fence we stand, we cannot fail to be impressed by the predator's ability to survive, and by its adaptability to changes in habitats.

SMALL MAMMALS

Hedgerows, copses and arable land support high densities of small animals, ranging from the tiny pigmy shrew to mice, voles and rats. Despite the abundance of these animals, they are notoriously difficult to observe and even more so to photograph. Both of these shots were taken in captivity where the animals were introduced into a ready-made set.

COMMON SHREW ▷

During feeding sessions, which must take place at least every two hours, the shrew is constantly on the move, pushing its inquistive snout into every likely place where insects might be found. The shrew does not lose its appetite in winter. In fact, in hard weather, the need for food increases. It will make its living through the colder winter months by searching for insects under decomposing organic debris, like leaf litter or in compost heaps.

◁ FIELD VOLE

The field vole is exclusively vegetarian in its feeding behaviour, living on a diet of fresh grass shoots and the foliage of low-growing hedgerow plants. Like other diurnal animals of open country, the field vole has developed a rapid breeding programme to offset the effects of its predators.

BUTTERFLIES

Butterflies are often considered as 'indicator species' when it comes to habitat quality assessment. In many species, the habitat requirement for the caterpillar may be completely different from that of the adult butterfly. Because of the effects of man's activities on the fragile habitats of these insects, it is likely that other species will eventually follow the Large Blue butterfly into the history books.

CHALKHILL BLUES ▷

Butterfly photography is seldom easy, simply due to the need to be close enough to the insect. It is best to attempt stalking butterflies in cool weather when they are less eager to fly. The shot of the chalkhill blues was taken at Fontmell Down on a July evening as the insects gathered in a valley to obtain maximum warmth from the sinking sun.

◁ SPECKLED WOOD

WETLANDS

From the hilly landscape of the South West, streams and rivers flow down into lakes, reservoirs and estuaries. These inland waterways act as a magnet for wildlife, with many species depending upon water as a main habitat in which to make a living. The fauna of rivers and lakes differs greatly from that of the coast, as many wetland species have specific habitat requirements.

◁ WATERSMEET

DIPPER ▷

The dipper is typical of fast-flowing rivers and streams, and may be seen throughout the hillier areas of the Wessex region. The name dipper is derived from the bird's habit of dipping up and down while standing on rocks in rapid water.

KINGFISHER

It was the kingfisher that inspired me to embark upon a career in nature photography. I had been watching a pair of these fabulous birds in their early stages of breeding on the River Asker, near Bridport. In the hope of sharing this experience with my family and friends, I rushed out and purchased a 35mm camera and a telephoto lens. That was in 1976 and I have been photographing wildlife ever since.

I never tire of photographing this gorgeous bird. These pictures were taken from a hide in the vicinity of a nest site on the River Brit.

HERON

E volution has moulded this bird into an efficient and adaptable killer of the marshes. The heron's long legs enable the bird to wade into deep water, where it will use its pickaxe-like bill to strike prey such as small fish, frogs, tadpoles, small mammals or birds, reptiles, molluscs and insects with deadly accuracy. Probably the bird's greatest attribute is its endless patience, standing motionless at the edge of a lake or pond for hours at a time, watching for signs of movement in the water.

D espite its large size, the heron is wary of man and is difficult to approach. These photographs were taken from a hide on the bank of a private lake in Dorset. Over 150 hours were spent in the hide before these pictures were obtained.

◁ HERON

MUTE SWAN

The mute swans of Abbotsbury and The Fleet make some of the most fabulous wildlife spectacles in Britain. In fact, Abbotsbury is the only place in the world where over 100 pairs of mute swans, nesting gregariously, are on view to the public. At any one time, several hundred swans may be present, especially at feeding time. The main shot here is of swans following the swanherd, who is carrying their feed bucket!

It would of course be most satisfying to photograph unusual species of wildlife on every assignment, but in reality, most birds and animals are impossible to approach with a camera without careful preparation beforehand. In most cases we have to settle for pictures of the commonplace, while being ever watchful for unusual poses!

COOT ▷

Observing bird behaviour can certainly help when it comes to predicting photogenic poses. From experience, I knew that there was a very good chance that this coot would stretch its wings as it preened at the water's edge in Weymouth Harbour. Predicting this shot, I quietly moved to the most suitable angle and patiently waited for the bird to perform.

◁ CANADA GOOSE

I had been watching this Canada goose preening for some time. The sun was striking the bird from the side, creating complimentary shadow detail – but its head was buried in its plumage! When it looked up I took the shot, just as the highlight of the sun came into the bird's eye.

TUFTED DUCK ▷

The tufted duck is a common species found on estuaries and lakes in the region. It is a relatively easy bird to approach, but the duck's pied plumage demands special lighting. I took this photograph on a sunny day at Sutton Bingham Reservoir. Although the duck is the main focal point, it is the breeze rippling the water which has created this dappled effect, with reflections that really make the picture work.

◁ POCHARD

Wherever there is water there will be ducks, especially in winter when birds move south to take advantage of a milder climate. The pochard is a typical wintering duck to be seen on lakes or reservoirs. This photograph is of a female drinking.

GREAT CRESTED GREBE ▷

T he picture of the great crested grebe was taken with great patience and persistence by stalking the bird on a Devon reservoir. The little grebe was photographed as it broke water with a stickleback on a pond in East Devon. This species proved to be too nervous to stalk and it was necessary to use a hide for this shot.

◁ LITTLE GREBE

B oth species of grebe shown here are found on inland waterways in the South West. They are diving birds, sustaining a living by catching small fish under water. Grebes can stay under water for up to a minute at a time and can cover considerable distances, which makes it impossible to predict where they will surface!

BEARDED TIT ▷

The bearded tit is specific to well managed reedbeds. It is a resident species at the Radipole Lake RSPB Nature Reserve in Weymouth. The best opportunities for seeing this exotic looking bird occur in late winter, when it feeds on reed seeds in small flocks. This was one of those rare lucky moments when I happened to be in the right place, at the right time! Half concealed by a small hawthorn bush, I waited quietly as a small party of birds worked their way towards me as they fed on the reed heads. I managed to obtain two quick shots of this male before he noticed me and took flight.

◁ COMMON SANDPIPER

The common sandpiper turns up at inland lakes in the South West during its spring and autumn passage. I attracted this bird to my hide at a lake in Dorset by placing a mirror at the water's edge. When the bird first noticed its reflection, it displayed vigorously to the mirror! It soon became relaxed, remaining in the vicinity of the mirror, feeding and preening for the rest of the day – presumably having gained additional confidence by the apparent presence of another bird nearby!

GRASS SNAKE

This is the largest reptile found in the South West. Adult females can grow up to 1.8 metres in length, but usually will measure 90–120 centimetres long. Grass snakes occur wherever their prey of frogs, toads and newts is abundant. Photographing them in the wild is a hit and miss affair and is seldom successful. These shots were taken of an adult, after catching the reptile near a garden at Hinton St.George, Somerset.

The grass snake is harmless to man, but when captured, displays an extraordinary series of defence routines. Its first line of defence is to exude a potent smelly liquid, which is so repulsive that the captor may immediately release the snake! If that does not work, it will feign death by lying motionless on its back with mouth open and tongue lolling. Finally, if the snake is still captive, it will regurgitate its most recent meal, which might be a partly digested frog or toad!

The most reliable opportunities of watching frogs and toads present themselves in late winter, when these animals move in large numbers to their spawning ponds to breed. I have lost count of the number of times I have accidentally slipped into the water in the quest for frog photos!

COMMON FROG ▷

Both of these photographs were contrived by gently coaxing the subjects into favourable positions. The chances of encountering a frog or toad posing in this way would be extremely remote!

◁ TOAD

DRAGONFLIES

With every aspect of wildlife photography there is always an 'if' and a 'but', and dragonflies are no exception to this rule. They are fascinating insects and can make superb subjects IF the photographer can get close enough, BUT usually they fly away! Nature photographers often talk in terms of 'fear zones' when referring to subjects. A fear zone is the distance from a given subject, at which it will not happily tolerate the approach of a photographer in the wild. Most self-respecting dragonflies have large fear zones and will take flight as soon as the photographer steps towards them. To overcome this problem, it is necessary to attempt dragonfly photography in conditions where they will not be eager to fly – like in the early morning or after a heavy storm of rain, when they will be waterlogged! Even then, they seem to be able to take off just before the exposure is made! This type of photography is truly a trial of patience!

SOUTHERN HAWKER DRAGONFLY ▷

◁ BEAUTIFUL DEMOISELLE

U p until around 5,000 years ago, undisturbed ancient forest covered the whole of Southern Britain. When man settled here in earnest, he began to change this wild woodland habitat to a landscape more suited to his own needs. The erosion of this natural habitat has continued to the present time. Even the largest native woodlands today are only tiny fragments of the great forest of which they once formed a part.

◁ NEW FOREST

JAY ▷

I n late summer, jays collect vast quantities of acorns and either store them in hollow trees or bury them for winter provisions. It is the bird's habit of burying acorns which made this flamboyant member of the crow family responsible for spreading the oak into Britain at the time of early afforestation. These hidden treasures are often forgotten by the birds, giving rise to the giant oaks of the future.

WOODPECKERS

In late winter, the characteristic drumming of the great spotted woodpecker echoes through woods and copses. This far-carrying sound is made by the male hammering his beak on a favourite resounding bough, and forms part of the birds' prenuptial display. Woodpeckers have evolved a unique niche in woodland ecology by pecking insect larvae from decaying timber. They are shy birds and will not tolerate the presence of humans, both of these photographs were taken from a hide. The male great spotted woodpecker was enticed to my garden with melted suet, which had been pushed into cracks and holes in the log, whereas the green woodpecker was photographed at the nest in a small copse in Somerset.

◁ GREEN WOODPECKER

GREAT SPOTTED WOODPECKER ▷

TAWNY OWL

After dark, the presence of this nocturnal hunter may be given away by the owl's haunting call – a long, quavering hoot. The tawny owl feeds on small woodland animals like mice and voles which it takes on silent wing.

These photographs were taken at a tawny owl nest site, in a small copse near my home. On one occasion, while the chicks were still in the nest, the hen owl arrived at the tree carrying a woodmouse. It was just past midnight, and as I leaned forward in excitement, my portable seat creaked, attracting the bird's attention. An hour later as I emerged from my hide, the adult owl attacked me. The only warning I received was the sudden rush of air as the bird's powerful talons struck me in the face!

With head down, clutching an array of tripods, flashguns and camera, I scurried away from the nest site, the angry mother owl flying around my head! As I cleaned my wounds at home, I felt honoured to have actually made contact with a wild tawny owl in flight, but on reflection, realised that this could have been a dangerous pastime!

◁ TAWNY OWL FLEDGELING

PHEASANT

In many species of bird, plumage colouration and markings vary dramatically between the sexes to suit the roles they perform. The common pheasant is a prime example of such variation. The female has dull, mottled markings, forming good camouflage for the bird to blend into her surroundings when incubating eggs or tending young. The handsome male boasts striking colours, which are used to full effect when displaying to a rival cock or a potential mate, as shown on the left. While watching the cock in the main photograph through my viewfinder, I anticipated his behaviour. As he stretched up and raised his wings in full display, I pressed the button on my motordrive to take a rapid succession of exposures, in order to secure the shot.

COCK PHEASANT ▷

◁ PAIR OF PHEASANTS

SONGTHRUSH AT NEST ▷

The sudden appearance of a hide near a nest can cause such distress to adult birds, they may desert their eggs or young. To prevent this from happening, it is vital to introduce a hide carefully in stages, slowly moving it nearer to the nest, thus allowing the birds to become accustomed to it. Once a hide is in place, it should be left for a further few days before photography can commence. Most songbirds are unable to count above two, and will usually behave normally when three people enter a hide and two of them come out and walk away. Even then, it is still important not to attempt to take photographs until the adults have made several visits to the nest. If the birds do not immediately relax into natural behaviour, the photographic session should be abandoned.

◁ BLACKBIRD

I took this photograph of a cock blackbird in full song after observing the bird using this particular perch on several occasions. A twenty foot high scaffold tower with a small hide on top was erected near the tree. Even after the hide had been in place for over a week, it still took a total of 16 hours waiting before the blackbird obliged!

WOODLAND

BADGER ▷

In the descending darkness of twilight, as the daytime birds and animals settle down to rest, it is time for the nightshift to take over in the woods. The badger is strictly nocturnal in its habits, emerging from its woodland home under cover of darkness, and venturing out into clearings, meadows and even gardens to search for its favourite food – earthworms. Badger cubs are born in late winter in an underground den, the adults becoming more predictable in their emergence times. This shot of a young badger leaving its earth was taken in a copse near Crewkerne, Somerset. It was necessary to use flash, so the equipment was left near the earth nightly for several evenings, to let the animals grow accustomed to the whine of the flashguns.

◁ WEASEL

Good wildlife photographs are seldom easy to obtain, and this weasel proved no exception! A total of 215 hours were spent on this subject before a single exposure was taken. The animal was tracked in the wild and eventually captured and introduced into a specially prepared photographic set. Despite the subject being in captivity, realistic photographs are still difficult to achieve. The key to success in this line of photography is in preparing the set, arranging sympathetic lighting and exercising endless patience while waiting for the animal to perform!

Although not impossible, it would be impractical to attempt to photograph small nocturnal mammals in wild and free conditions. For both these shots, a special photographic box was constructed, incorporating a black backcloth to give a nocurnal effect, and a plate glass front. The woodland scene in both cases took hours to prepare.

WOODMOUSE ▷

The woodmouse was caught in a live catching trap and introduced into the set. The animal has been exposed by three flashguns, each positioned to achieve near natural lighting.

◁ HEDGEHOG

The hedgehog was found one morning curled up in my garage in early October. It was gently lifted into the box and photographed as it became active at dusk.

FALLOW DEER ▷

In mid October, the rutting season for fallow deer reaches its peak. At this time, mature bucks may be heard barking from deep within the woods as they warn other bucks away from their own harem of does. The extraordinary grunting call of the fallow buck can only be described as something between a belch and a snort!

◁ GREY SQUIRREL

This agile mammal is present in woodlands throughout the South West. It is not a native of this country, but was introduced by man from North America. These photographs were taken from a hide, where the grey squirrel appeared to take no notice of human scent and was not bothered by the sound of a loud motordrive. I attracted this squirrel to acorns which had been collected in autumn and offered to the squirrels in early winter.

BUTTERFLIES

Woodland rides and clearings are perfect places in which to watch butterflies in the summer months. The brimstone butterfly overwinters in evergreen foliage. Hence the process of evolution has provided this insect with distinct leaf-shaped wings. On the first warm days of March, it comes dancing along the woodland rides like a blur of sulphur yellow. The silver-washed fritillary is one the largest woodland butterflies to be seen in the South West, usually in areas of mature deciduous trees, where it may be found feeding on bramble. Sadly, the heath fritillary is no longer common. It is a woodland species, preferring open, young stands of trees. In the Wessex region, it may now be found only in a few scattered and isolated locations in Devon.

BRIMSTONE ▷

SILVER-WASHED FRITILLARY ▽

HEATH FRITILLARY ▽

HORNET ▷

The South West of England has always been a stronghold for this formidable insect. Although awesome in appearance, it is a docile insect and seldom uses its potent sting away from the nest. This queen flew into my living room one September morning. I apprehended her and kept her in a dark, cool container till dusk, then gently tipped her out on to this log for a short photographic session before she flew off.

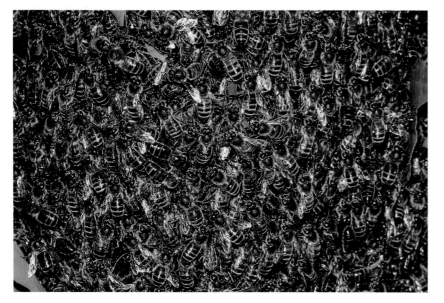

◁ BEE SWARM

When the old queen leaves the nest in spring, she takes the majority of worker bees with her. At first, she settles on a branch and the workers cling to her, often making a massive cluster of bees the size of a rugby ball. I tried to approach this swarm in the daytime, but they became agitated by my presence. Returning at dusk, I found their fear zone greatly reduced and was able to approach within two feet of the swarm for this shot, exposed with flash.

ORB SPINNER ▷

Spider webs are unique feats of engineering, built to withstand the shock of airborne insects colliding with the gossamer. These insect traps can be wonderfully photogenic in the low morning or evening light. This picture was taken near a garden pond in September early evening sunlight, just as the spider had completed spinning the web.

◁ DUNG FLY

The very name of this insect suggests an association with manure, and whilst it does lay its eggs on dung, it is in fact a woodland predator! The dung fly catches prey in flight by using its long, bristly legs to arrest the unfortunate victim. This insect was stalked with a 50mm macro lens to achieve a life-size image. The exposure was made with flash.

The forging of the Wessex coastline by the south westerly gales is a continuing process. These powerful winds whip the sea into a violent force, capable of making dramatic changes to the coastal landscape literally overnight.

The distinct change in habitat between land and sea makes the coast richer in terms of variety of wildlife than any inland wilderness. Here, landbirds rub shoulders with ocean-going species, and the tideline attracts an ever-changing procession of waders.

THE FLEET, DORSET ▷

◁ EAST CLIFF, WEST BAY, DORSET

HERRING GULL ▷

The herring gull is the most frequently seen member of the gull family on the South West coast. It is a noisy, boisterous bird which has adapted well to man's buildings near the sea where it often nests on rooftops. I stalked this bird on the east cliff at West Bay. It became restless as I approached, and as the bird slipped from the ledge, I released my shutter to catch the wings in this raised position.

◁ FULMAR

The fulmar petrel nests on sheer cliff faces and islands in the South West in spring. It is an impressive bird in flight, wheeling and soaring on the air currents with a stiff-winged motion. During the nesting season the fulmar habitually winnows against the cliff faces, instigating a cackling chorus from sitting birds. This photograph was taken from the beach at Beer in Devon. Using a hand-held camera, I followed the bird in flight until it came into sharp focus directly above me.

BLACK HEADED GULL ▷

The black headed gull might be more aptly named 'brown headed gull', as the bird's head becomes a dark chocolate brown colour in the breeding season. This photograph was taken from a hide overlooking a lagoon on Brownsea Island. The exposure was made just as the bird lowered its head to drink. The pose of the gull, together with its reflection, suggests an attitude of vanity.

◁ LESSER BLACK BACKED GULL

The continuing success of the lesser black backed gull has caused concern among ornithologists, for this gull is a predator of eggs and young of smaller birds. In some areas, control is carried out by reducing clutch sizes of the gull to lessen the effect of predation on more vulnerable species. At the nest, the lesser black backed gull will defend its eggs or young with great determination. Only seconds after I made this exposure of a threatening adult near the nest, the bird attacked me from the air!

CORMORANT ▷

A fishing cormorant is a peculiar sight, for all that can be seen of the bird is its head and neck, giving the impression that the bird is sinking. Under water, the cormorant outswims its prey, and to do this effectively, the bird lacks the degree of oil in its plumage which gives other water birds buoyancy. This species may be seen anywhere around the South West coast, often standing on a rock or post, its wings outstretched to dry after a prolonged fishing session.

◁ PUFFIN

The puffin is an ocean-going bird, spending nine months of the year on the high seas. It ventures on to land only in the breeding season, when it nests in underground burrows. Sadly, this species has declined dramatically in the South West, and may only be seen with reliable frequency on offshore islands and at a few scattered locations on the mainland.

AVOCET ▷

The success of the avocet as a British breeding species is due in the first place to careful habitat management on the east coast by conservation organisations such as the RSPB. This success is reflected in the large numbers of avocets which can be seen during the winter in the South West. The Exe Estuary and Brownsea Island are two notable wintering sites for this bird.

◁ SANDWICH TERNS

The sandwich tern is a summer visitor, arriving in the South West during spring, when it nests on undisturbed shingle. I took this shot of four sandwich terns at the Fleet Nature Reserve near Abbotsbury in Dorset.

RINGED PLOVER ▷

The distinct markings of the ringed plover act as highly effective camouflage, causing the bird to literally vanish into the pebble beaches where it nests. The bird becomes conspicuous however, when feeding on sand or mudflats with other waders. I obtained this photograph on the Chesil Beach near Portland, after watching a pair of ringed plovers displaying in early spring. Lying on the pebbles between two upturned boats, I waited patiently for one of the birds to venture close enough for the shot.

◁ REDSHANK

Photographing waders can be a frustrating business. The usual technique is to sit in a hide on a sandbank or mudflat, in the hope that the birds will come close enough to photograph, which unfortunately, more often than not they don't! I was watching this bird at rest through my lens, when a flock of oystercatchers flew piping overhead. The redshank stretched itself upwards in this alert posture, which it maintained just long enough for me to make the exposure.

STONECHAT ▷

Although typically found on heathland, the stonechat is equally at home in dense thickets of gorse or blackthorn near the coast. The handsome cockbird characteristically stands on a favourite perch, uttering clicking notes as it scolds passing walkers. This alarm call resembles the sound of two pebbles being knocked together, hence the name stonechat. I took this photograph of a male stonechat from a small portable hide positioned near a stand of gorse on the landslip west of Lyme Regis.

◁ JACKDAW

As a hole-nesting member of the crow family, the jackdaw exploits the availability of suitable holes in cliff faces, and the abundance of food to be found at seaside towns. This picture was taken in Weymouth Harbour, where the bird had learned that food thrown frequently to the ducks might easily come his way.

SLOW WORM ▷

Dry scrub and grassland on coastal cliffs and landslips are excellent sites for watching reptiles. The slow worm is in fact a lizard without legs. I found this individual dozing under a piece of tin on cliffs near Lyme Regis.

◁ ADDER

The adder is our only venomous reptile. This snake was photographed at West Bexington. While I was crawling through the undergrowth in my attempt to get close enough to the subject, I heard what I first thought to be dry grass rustling in the breeze. It turned out to be another adder hissing at me, a distance of only six inches from my ear!